# DOGS FOR
# PROTECTION

# DOGS FOR
# PROTECTION

by Lucine Hansz Flynn

**Title page photo:** Rob Lumsden, Clarksburg, Md., with the family Collie.

Special thanks are owed to Irene and Milton Weidler. At a critical moment and on short notice they joined in the preparation of this book and gave generously of their expertise, their time, their enthusiasm, including their outstanding photographs, which include all of the black and white photos (except photo on page 26) and some of the color photos appearing in the book.

ISBN 0-87666-813-9

Distributed in the UNITED STATES by T.F.H. Publications, Inc., 211 West Sylvania Avenue, Neptune City, NJ 07753; in CANADA by H & L Pet Supplies Inc., 27 Kingston Crescent, Kitchener, Ontario N2B 2T6; Rolf C. Hagen Ltd., 3225 Sartelon Street, Montreal 382 Quebec; in ENGLAND by T.F.H. (Great Britain) Ltd., 11 Ormside Way, Holmethorpe Industrial Estate, Redhill, Surrey RH1 2PX; in AUSTRALIA AND THE SOUTH PACIFIC by T.F.H. (Australia) Pty. Ltd., Box 149, Brookvale 2100 N.S.W., Australia; in NEW ZEALAND by Ross Haines & Son, Ltd., 18 Monmouth Street, Grey Lynn, Auckland 2 New Zealand; in SINGAPORE AND MALAYSIA by MPH Distributors Pte., 71-77 Stamford Road, Singapore 0617; in the PHILIPPINES by Bio-Research, 5 Lippay Street, San Lorenzo Village, Makati, Rizal; in SOUTH AFRICA by Multipet Pty. Ltd., 30 Turners Avenue, Durban 4001. Published by T.F.H. Publications Inc., Ltd., the British Crown Colony of Hong Kong.

# CONTENTS

Nancy McCary, Rockville, Md., and her Viszla guide dog Paddy
perfecting their technique in working together.

# Why a Dog?

You've got to *do* something. In the last three months there have been seven break-ins within less than a mile of home. One man had the license plates stolen off his car, and the thieves came right into his carport to do it. And that poor soul three doors down—she wasn't away from home more than twenty minutes, but when she came back and opened her kitchen door she was face to face with a total stranger, big and mean-looking. She had the mother wit to scream and run to a neighbor, but she hasn't got over the shock yet.

Clearly, you've got to do something. You've already thought of moving somewhere else, but where would you go? Besides, long conferences around the kitchen table have made it abundantly plain that moving costs too much. Besides again, except for feeling intermittently unsafe, you like it where you are. It's home.

You've thought of getting a gun. But you don't really *want* a gun. You don't know anything about guns; furthermore, you don't want to know. You're afraid of guns, all of them, right down to children's cap pistols. Getting a gun has no appeal at all.

Still . . . You've got to do *something*.

### Dogs Are Good Protection
What you need is a dog. For your purposes, a dog can be better than a gun. Not just any dog, but almost any dog.

No?

Ah, but think it through.

It's true that you can't take a dog with you every-where you go; some places exclude dogs. But there

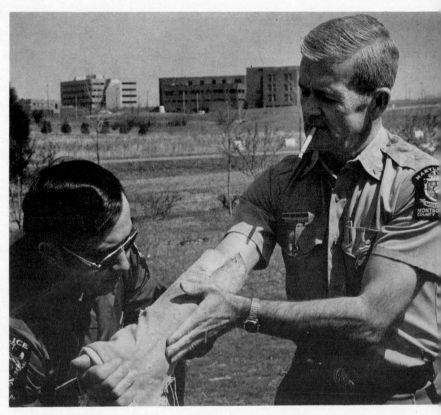

Officer William Wilhelm wraps heavy canvas around Sgt. Joseph McGrogan's arm in preparation for a practice attack. The Sergeant then puts on a jacket to conceal the wrappings from Major.

are many more places you can't take a gun. In some jurisdictions it's already illegal even to own a gun without first getting a permit that is not easy to come by, and most places have ordinances against carrying a gun. The frontier was closed some years ago, and the day of strapping on your weapon as a part of getting dressed is gone.

A former chief of police of Washington, D.C. has been quoted to the effect that to his knowledge dog-walkers had never been attacked while out with their dogs. Sergeant Joseph W. McGrogan, head of the Montgomery County (Md.) Police Department's K-9 program, distrusts absolutes and would not go so far. "Never say never," quoted the sergeant. He agreed, though, that a dog on the spot was better than a gun that was somewhere else, although the degree of that favorable margin could not be quantified. Some things don't lend themselves to expression in numbers.

Sergeant McGrogan added that even if you had your gun with you, it might not be any advantage. Guns, he explained, can be taken away—he made the taking sound like child's play—so that, "You can end up being shot with your own gun." The sergeant brooded for a moment over the vision he had conjured. Then he brightened. "Your dog," he said, "can't be turned against you."

Having a dog on your side lengthens the odds in your favor—much or little, depending on your dog and your situation. The advantage, again, cannot be quantified, but it should not for that reason be despised, even when the difference might appear to be marginal.

For one who wants a dog to go along on the street for protection, Sergeant McGrogan pointed out that a dog of good substance is more likely to deter potential assailants than one smaller or more fragile in appearance. Basenjis and Whippets, for example, are both hounds approximately equal in height, but the heavier-bodied Basenji is more impressive-looking than the slimmer, more finely-boned Whippet. Both breeds, in fact, make good watchdogs. In turn, the Whippet, being taller, might look like more dog than, say, the Shih Tzu, a very hairy toy breed gaining in popularity in recent years, even though the Shih Tzu could weigh almost as much as the Whippet.

The question is not solely how much dog do you have with you, but how much dog is perceived by someone else. A tiny toy dog "on its little velvet lead," in the sergeant's graphic phrase, is not likely to instill much deterring awe in anybody, and good common sense prompts assent to his thesis. Given a choice between a very small dog and a bigger one to go along to the bank with the day's receipts, take the bigger dog. If your choice, however, is between either a very small dog to go for a walk in the afternoon or no dog at all, take the toy along.

But leave the velvet lead and rhinestone collar at home. Toys aren't the only breeds to wear them. Get your dog a plain leather collar. If yours is a little dog, incidentally, and you're having trouble finding a collar small enough, ask to see collars meant for cats. Get a plain lead. Any dog so equipped at once looks more as if it really *can* protect something.

Similarly, use a little discretion in naming your dog, no matter what its size. If part of your purpose in keeping a dog is protection, don't give it a name that suggests silliness to a listener. Beowulf, not Sweetums. There's nothing wrong with browsing through a dictionary of given names for ideas. Timothy, Rachel, Max, Gretchen are a few examples that come readily to mind. All are in use as the call names of living dogs.

To be sure, an element of play-acting and a degree of bluff enter into all this, and it could work out that your Silky Terrier, who answers to Wotan as he accompanies you on his plain collar and lead, may be roughly equivalent to an empty gun. But there is always an element of doubt whether the gun really is empty. When it's pointed at you, doubt suddenly grows very large, with urgent second thoughts to crowd the mind.

Those second thoughts are just what you're trying to engender. Maybe you're play-acting and maybe you aren't. There is the doubt grounded in the best of all possible reasons: no one, least of all a stranger, really can predict what a dog will do. Through the millenia dogs have shown themselves ready in

Major in attack. With all the preparation, the Sergeant still got bitten. Major's teeth went through the sleeve and all the padding.

defense—big, tough, scrappy dogs, and also, unpredictably, the unlikely ones. The gentlest, softest-mouthed bird dogs and, yes, the toys, in moments of truth have been as willing to fight and die as any Mastiff that ever set foot to ground.

Get yourself a dog, then, of reasonable size if you expect to take it around with you, and go your way with a confident air. A stranger seeing your dog move along beside you on a loose lead might even jump to conclusions. That dog, he might decide, looks as if he's had attack training. Better leave that one alone.

11

This dog was on duty when the picture was taken. The warning sign is to be taken seriously.

# How About an Attack Dog? Or a Guard Dog?

Having come this far in considering your protection problem, you might think that the thing to do is simply to go all out and get an attack or guard dog and be done with it. The dog will know what to do; that's what he's trained for. No more problem.

This seductive reasoning is false. Most emphatically, you don't want such a dog, you only momentarily think you do. Most emphatically, do not attempt to get such a dog. Far from seeing your problems in protecting you and yours come to a speedy end, an appalling realization would shortly break over you that those problems had only just begun.

Before considering why this is true—and it is true on several counts—it might be well to clarify a confusion of terms between "attack dog" and "guard dog." Add to this that "security dog," "police dog" (meaning here not a breed, but any dog that does police work), and "man-stopper" are sometimes used instead of "attack dog," while "plant protection dog," "security dog" again, and "watchdog" are substituted for "guard dog." People at large use all these terms to mean pretty much the same thing, so confusion multiplies. Among professional dog trainers the words are not synonyms. Whatever names they use, professionals divide these specially trained dogs into two broad groups, those that work with a handler and those that work alone.

The dogs' levels of training are different. Dogs trained to work with a handler hold the canine equivalent of college degrees. They have been given the most, and the most sophisticated, training to do the greatest variety of tasks. Here the police dogs are trained to attack and subdue malefactors, to control crowds, to smell out drugs and bombs and whatnot. Here also, in more peaceful endeavor, are found guide dogs for the blind and dogs to aid the deaf. Although not intended primarily as protection, both guide dogs and dogs for the deaf, by their presence and training, make the world safer as well as more pleasant and convenient for their people.

Next down the academic scale—call them dogs with high-school diplomas—are dogs that work alone, chiefly to guard warehouses, commercial and industrial yards, department stores and the like, at night or other off hours when the legitimate human occupants are gone. These dogs are conditioned to friendship with one or preferably two people but trained to attack indiscriminately anyone else entering their areas, protecting themselves the while against counterattack by the interlopers.

Neither guard nor attack dogs are so plentiful as to be easy to find, and they cannot be used interchangeably. Further, only a minority among dogs can be trained to attack or guard work. In a very real sense, these are the superdogs, even before training, possessing the essential combination of intelligence and correct temperament, a combination that must be inborn. It cannot be taught. Of the two elements, intelligence is easier found. Many dogs with sufficient intelligence to learn the tasks set them will fail their training course. Their failure is a matter of faulty temperament.

Many people have a notion that a big dog with a nasty temperament will make a good "police dog." He's big— anyone can see that—and he's naturally mean, always aggressive, a vicious biter. Anyone will soon find that out. What more could be wanted? A good many such dogs are offered to police departments here and there as gifts. What better way to get

Do not try to train a dog to look menacing as an empty threat. K-9 Major of the Montgomery County (Md.) Police Department threatens in earnest.

rid of them? Well, the police don't want them either. Of dogs offered to Montgomery County, Maryland, as candidates, only about ten percent are accepted for the K-9 corps.

The temperament required for attack or guard training could scarcely be more different from popular supposition. What's needed is a dog that is essentially an amiable and sweet-tempered dog yet sufficiently aggressive to benefit from the training and not cave in under it. These antithetical traits must be present in a mix of extraordinary stability, coupled with a strong innate sense of responsibility. Dogs with all those facets to their temperaments are in short supply; so are qualified instructors for their training.

Attack dogs and guard dogs are not trained in a week-end in somebody's spare time. Training is ar-

Guide dog Kia, a black Labrador Retriever, stops at the curb for her mistress, Jane Carona, Bladensburg, Md., saving her from what could be a nasty fall.

duous, intensive and long-continued. It is no task for an enthusiastic amateur to embark upon, book in hand. The dedicated do-it-yourselfer had best turn his energies in some other direction. Enthusiasm aside, most people managing busy schedules cannot give the time required for training such a dog. Police dogs in Montgomery County are brought back to the training academy every two weeks for a refresher course, so their training truly never ends. Most people have other things to do.

You might think to circumvent the problem of training by simply buying a dog already trained. In that case, be prepared to spend thousands of dollars. Be prepared, further, to make the most searching investigation of the dog's training. Who trained it? What are the trainer's qualifications? (Teaching a few classes of basic obedience to pets and their owners is not sufficient.) What methods did he use? Who are his customers? Check every statement and take nothing for granted. Keep in mind while you're checking that nothing is true merely because someone says it is true, be it said ever so sincerely. Check with your local police, with the Better Business Bureau, with any consumer protection agencies operating in your area. Seek out local dog people; dog people are gossipy about their interest. Take your time. What you're looking for is information from independent, unrelated sources about this trainer and his dogs, whether the reports be good or ill.

If this caution sounds excessive, there is good reason for it. While competently and adequately trained attack or guard dogs are in short supply, there are others around in greater numbers whose training has been fearfully misguided. "Fearful" is the correct word. Such dogs are dangerous.

Be its schooling of the finest, however, any attack dog can be dangerous in the company of an unskilled handler. That point is important enough to bear restatement: **the handler of an attack dog must be trained as carefully as the dog**. Police handlers of attack dogs should be chosen and trained as meticulously as the dogs. By no means do all who apply gain the assignment. Attack dogs can be triggered into action, innocently and inadvertently, far easier than they can be stopped. Unless the handler is trained, someone is likely to be maimed or killed.

Sergeant McGrogan seemed to find the spectacle of an unskilled citizenry running about with attack dogs as depressing as the idea of the same citizenry going abroad armed with guns. When asked specifically about the disadvantages of keeping an attack or guard dog, the sergeant's first response was, "Have they checked on their liability insurance?" You can almost depend on being sued, when sympathies would almost as surely run against you.

For your purposes, forget about attack dogs and guard dogs. Forget also the notion of trying to instill in a dog just a *little* training for attack, with the idea that it will look or act more intimidating without doing any actual harm. The dog will only be made erratic, and therefore doubly dangerous, in its responses. Nor is the danger solely what the dog might do to a potentially threatening stranger. Your dog might decide that now is the time it doesn't feel like playing tough dog, leaving you without a show of force when you need it.

Your needs can be taken care of by a good family dog, one that will afford you protection largely just by being there. Your dog's ears and nose are far keener than yours, and they are always on duty. At home or away, your dog's senses provide a splendid early warning system, enabling you to take sensible action in your own behalf. You can't, after all, reasonably expect your dog to assume *all* responsibility for your safety.

What are you to make, then, of the jokes about the family dog that obliges the burglar in the friendliest

Among other things, dogs for the deaf during training are taught to pick up items dropped. Liebe recovers a dropped wallet. German Shepherds are not typical dogs for the deaf; usually, mixed breeds under 40 lbs. are used.

way by leading him to the silver chest? Well, often they are jokes and nothing more. Or the dog could have received some unintentional reverse training. For example, if you rebuke your dog every time it barks at visitors, it may in time believe that you want *every* caller made welcome. Instead, you need a small ritual of presenting guests to your dog, and vice versa, to convey to the dog that only those visitors presented with the ritual are all right. One family, for instance, taught their dogs to sit near the door and to stay there until guests could enter, take off outer wraps, and be seated; not before then would the dogs be released with an "Okay" and allowed to approach the company for a greeting. Neighbors reported that when no one but the dogs was at home they raised an alarm, as they did when anyone came to the door unexpectedly.

Another guard dog, supplied by K-9 Security Co., Alexandria, Va. This is a Kuvasz, a large white Hungarian breed traditionally used in its native country as a guard dog.

Dogs do deter by their presence. Every now and then there will be a spate of "confession" type stories by burglars, whether reformed or merely in jail, saying that what they dreaded most during their rounds was a good, noisy dog. They ought to know.

There is a note sounded here of taking on faith. You hope your dog will perform in an emergency as you would want—while hoping at the same time that it's never put to the test. Exactly the same considerations apply to any insurance policy. Hoping that your house never burns down is a poor reason for neglecting to carry fire insurance.

Moreover, the recommendation against attack or guard dogs doesn't mean that your dog should have no schooling of any kind. You certainly should train your dog. But first you have to decide which dog to get.

# What Kind of Dog?

Once you decide to get a dog, you immediately are confronted by a question: what kind of dog should you get? The answer is that it's pretty much up to you. What appeals to you?

In the same breath with "what kind," people ask also whether they should look for a male dog or a female. Now, the males of any breed are not possessed of keener noses and sharper intelligence than the females of their breed, but they are somewhat larger and heavier than the females. Males are used exclusively in police work and guard duty, where extra weight and greater muscle could be decisive in a chancy situation. But that is not the primary reason why they are chosen for such work.

The reason is expediency. Females come into season, usually twice a year, and usually at an inconvenient time. The only sure way around this inconvenience is to have them spayed. Police departments avoid both inconvenience and expense simply by using males in their programs.

In your home, where you keep one dog as protector and companion, a female could serve you well. One woman said that the only time she ever felt herself in imminent danger—she was confronted suddenly by a potential aggressor keyed to a hair trigger—her dog, a female, took a quick reading of the situation and then stiffened her legs, lowered her head, and stuck her tail straight out behind her. She was ready. Another woman told of being much frightened, one day while at home alone, to look from her kitchen into her breezeway and see a strange man there. In the same instant the dog, bent on mayhem, cleared the bottom half of the divided door. Again the dog was a female.

It all comes down again to a question of preference. Males are sometimes naturally more aggressive than females of their breed. If this pleases you, or if their extra dollop of aggressiveness makes you feel more secure, then choose a male to protect your home. You should realize, however, that he may also be more given to roaming, and he'll be a sucker and a pushover for every female in season in the neighborhood, with "neighborhood" taking in a wider area than you would believe possible. Your female typically will be more of a homebody, while spaying is a one-time expense. It's good policy, though, to suffer with her through one season. Females who are spayed before their first season tend not to develop mature personalities, but rather to remain, psychologically, perpetual puppies.

For those who can be happy only with a purebred dog, the American Kennel Club (largest and best known, in the United States, of the dog registering organizations) at present recognizes around 130 breeds. Representatives of some breeds are fairly common; the Beagle, a smooth-coated hound popular for its medium size and ease of maintenance, is an example of a common breed. Representatives of many other breeds, such as the Australian Cattle Dog and Tibetan Spaniel, are more scarce. (The Australian Cattle Dog, also medium-sized and smooth-coated, is an energetic working dog, naturally suspicious of strangers, that needs a good deal of activity to thrive. Tibetan Spaniels are small, long-coated dogs used as watchdogs in their native Tibet. Long-lived and adaptable, they fit well as house dogs in varied family situations.)

A case can be made for ignoring purity of breeding and choosing a mongrel, and here is as good a place as any to point out that pure breeding is an all-or-nothing proposition. Dogs can't be just a little bit purebred any more than females, in the old joke, can be just a little bit pregnant. Those who breed a dog of one pure breed to a bitch of another pure breed do not thereby create a new breed; they create mongrels. The blow can be softened by calling the pups cross-breeds, but they're mongrels all the same.

Neither does it matter, as far as the registering associations are concerned, that pups resulting from

A group of 4-H members with their dogs before the obedience class begins. Every well-run obedience class should include a similar sociable time for dogs. The people usually enjoy it too.

such a breeding may be healthy, pretty, intelligent, and charming. Millions of dogs, whether first-generation crosses or of long, proud lineages certifiably indeterminate, possess all these attributes, as much as anyone could want.

And, they are available. Always and everywhere. From the bitch's misalliance down the block, from humane societies and other animal shelters, from the classified columns in the local newspaper, dogs can be found without much trouble and usually at little or no cost. Cherish your dog, then, and don't apologize for your choice.

One of the chief advantages of a purebred dog is the greater element of certainty in what you're getting. The pups turn out pretty much the same size and appearance and temperament as others of their breed. Mongrels are more of a gamble.

If you choose a purebred, you can expect to pay for your choice. How much you'll be asked to pay can range from just a few dollars to into the thousands, with the exact amount being determined mostly by the supply and demand for puppies of the breed you want and the seller's estimation of how good the puppy is. The point is that for not too much money you should be able to find a well-bred, healthy pup in any of a number of breeds. Older dogs sometimes go for more money, sometimes for less. Much depends on how the seller looks at things.

As a rule, there are several advantages in buying your dog from a breeder or other private owner, that is to say, direct from the source. Your questions may be answered more readily and more fully than is possible by a middleman. You can usually see the mother and sometimes the sire of the pup you are considering, along with other puppies in the litter, and form a first-hand impression of the breed. You can judge a pup's temperament far better by seeing it with littermates than by inspecting it alone in a cage.

Shopping for a dog calls for the same caution as shopping for anything else. Ask your questions *before* paying your money. Check with your Better Business Bureau. Inquire about the various sources of puppies in your area. See what you can find out about not only where puppies are sold but also the reputations of the sellers.

Do not let yourself be gulled by price differences between dogs offered for sale "with papers" and those "without papers." Registration with a national kennel club is what is meant, but the cost of registering a dog is nominal. The papers should go with the dog (whatever the price) at the time of the sale. This means that you should be given an application for registration with the national registry association (for most breeds in the United States the application will be made to the American Kennel Club, but for some it will be the United Kennel Club) properly filled out and signed by the seller, or a bill-of-sale or statement, likewise signed by the seller, containing full information to identify the dog. This includes the breed, color and sex of the dog; the registered names of both parents of the dog; the date of birth; and the name and address of the breeder. All of this information is needed for identification through the records.

Some people attach no importance to registration papers. Still, if you're buying a registrable dog, you might as well have the papers. You will need something in writing in case a dispute arises, and it is your responsibility to get that written something at the time you buy the dog. Promises of later delivery are not sufficient and should not be accepted.

### Breed Preferences

Probably you'll already have a breed preference in mind before you ever begin looking at dogs. In case you're undecided, however, here is a checklist of breeds you might want to consider—some known to all, some less familiar.

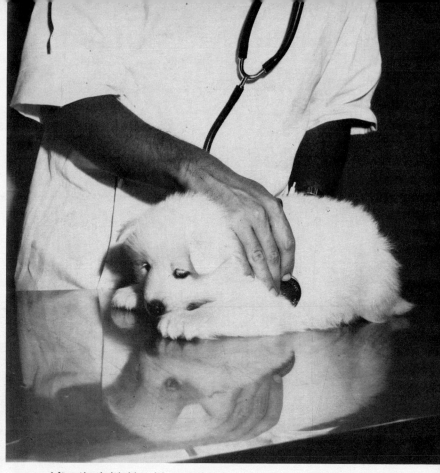

After the initial health examination of a new puppy, the veterinarian will prescribe a series of inoculations for the common diseases that affect most dogs. Photo by Louise van der Meid.

**Opposite page:** Registering a dog with the AKC takes place in three steps. First, the breeder applies to register the litter on a form supplied by the AKC. The AKC then issues an "AKC Dog Registration Application" for each puppy in the litter (top photo). This form should be filled with close attention to the instructions contained in it, front and back. When the "Registration Certificate" is issued, the dog's registration is complete (bottom photo).

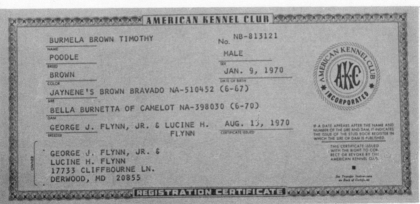

**AKC DOG REGISTRATION APPLICATION**
IF NOT USED RETURN TO AKC WITH EXPLANATION

BC  626

FOR OFFICE USE ONLY

FEE $5.00
DO NOT SEND CASH
Add $1.00 For Each
Supplemental Transfer

DOG'S NAME →

The person who owns this dog and applies to register it has the right to name it. Limit name to 25 letters. Print one letter per box - skip a box between words. Names are subject to AKC approval. AKC may assign a number suffix.

1ST CHOICE

2ND CHOICE

BREED SIBERIAN HUSKY

DATE OF BIRTH
OCT 5 1981

LITTER NUMBER WM815287

SIRE CH YETI'S BALTIC VIN   WD976189 (3-80)

DAM TANKASHA'S JOYFUL JUNO   WE491830 (3-82)

BREEDER JOAN C ZOETER

LITTER OWNER
JOAN C ZOETER
9408 SEVEN LOCKS RD
BETHESDA, MD 20817

NOV 20 1981
ISSUED

* The American Kennel Club Inc. 1976

INDICATE DOG'S SEX AND COLOR

Owner of Litter, indicate SEX ____
and circle the one letter below for the color which best describes this dog. If none apply enter color on last line.

A GRAY & WHITE
B BLACK & WHITE
C RED & WHITE

E SABLE & WHITE

G WHITE
H AGOUTI & WHITE
OTHER —

THE AKC RESERVES THE RIGHT TO CORRECT OR REVOKE FOR CAUSE ANY REGISTRATION CERTIFICATE ISSUED. ANY MISREPRESENTATION ON THIS APPLICATION IS CAUSE FOR CANCELLATION AND MAY RESULT IN LOSS OF ALL AKC PRIVILEGES FOR THOSE INDIVIDUALS WHO VIOLATE THE INTEGRITY OF THIS APPLICATION.

---

**INSTRUCTIONS:** PLEASE TYPE — OR USE PEN. NO PENCIL. Erasures or Corrections may cause return of application for an explanation.

**SEC. A** MUST BE COMPLETED IN FULL and SIGNED BY OWNER OF LITTER (AND CO-OWNER, IF ANY) SHOWN ON REVERSE SIDE.

ONE box MUST be checked
☐ I (we) still own this dog, and I (we) apply to The American Kennel Club to register it and have ownership recorded in my (our) name(s).
☐ I (we) certify that this dog was transferred DIRECTLY TO THE FOLLOWING PERSON(S) ON ____ mo. ____ day ____ year

MUST be filled in by owner(s) of Litter
PRINT NAME(S) OF PERSON(S) TO WHOM DOG WAS DIRECTLY TRANSFERRED ____
ADDRESS ____

Signature ____
OWNER OF LITTER AT BIRTH

Signature ____
CO-OWNER (IF ANY) OF LITTER AT BIRTH

**SEC. B** TO BE COMPLETED and SIGNED BY THE PERSON(S) NAMED IN SEC. A ABOVE, PROVIDED the person(s) owns the dog at the time this application is submitted to the A.K.C. If the person(s) named in SEC. A has transferred the dog to some other person(s), DO NOT COMPLETE SEC. B instead - obtain a Supplemental Transfer Statement form from the A.K.C. Instructions for its completion and use are on the form.

I apply to The American Kennel Club to have Registration Certificate for this dog issued in my/our name(s), and certify that I/we acquired it DIRECTLY from the person(s) who Signed Sec. A above, and that I/we still own this dog. I agree to abide by American Kennel Club rules and regulations.

New Owner's Signature ____
New Co-Owner's Signature ____

PRINT
Name ____
Address ____
City ____ State ____ Zip ____

PRINT
Name ____
Address ____
City ____ State ____ Zip ____

→ REGISTRATION FEE MUST ACCOMPANY APPLICATION. MAKE CHECKS, MONEY ORDERS PAYABLE TO THE AMERICAN KENNEL CLUB. DO NOT SEND STAMPS OR CASH.

FEE $5.00 plus $1.00 for each additional transfer of dog represented by Supplemental Transfer Statement. FEES SUBJECT TO CHANGE WITHOUT NOTICE

When completed and submitted, this Application becomes the property of the American Kennel Club
Mail to: THE AMERICAN KENNEL CLUB, 51 Madison Avenue, New York, N. Y. 10010

---

**AMERICAN KENNEL CLUB**

BURMELA BROWN TIMOTHY
NAME
POODLE
BREED
BROWN
COLOR

No. NB-813121

MALE
SEX
JAN. 9, 1970
DATE OF BIRTH

JAYNENE'S BROWN BRAVADO NA-510452 (6-67)
SIRE
BELLA BURNETTA OF CAMELOT NA-398030 (6-70)
DAM

GEORGE J. FLYNN, JR. & LUCINE H. FLYNN
BREEDER

AUG. 13, 1970
CERTIFICATE ISSUED

GEORGE J. FLYNN, JR. &
LUCINE H. FLYNN
17733 CLIFFBOURNE LN.
DERWOOD, MD 20855

IF A DATE APPEARS AFTER THE NAME AND NUMBER OF THE SIRE AND DAM, IT INDICATES THE ISSUE OF THE STUD BOOK REGISTER IN WHICH THE SIRE OR DAM IS PUBLISHED.

THIS CERTIFICATE ISSUED WITH THE RIGHT TO CORRECT OR REVOKE BY THE AMERICAN KENNEL CLUB.

See Transfer Instructions on Back of Certificate

**REGISTRATION CERTIFICATE**

27

Socialization continues after you bring your puppy home. Rides in the car help.

The German Shepherd is the breed of choice for police work in this country, so much so that "police dog" is a commonly understood synonym for the breed. When a guardian and protector are desired, the Shepherd comes to mind.

How often have you heard something along the lines of, "I'm gonna get me the biggest and meanest police dog I can find . . ." Unfortunately, big and mean ones can be found. The breed has suffered the usual fate of popularity in late years: careless and indiscriminate breeding. All too many German Shepherds now display unstable temperaments, making them unreliable and even dangerous to have around. Just remember that the big, mean police dog that bites everyone else is likely to bite you too, and your children, and to do serious damage.

In addition, German Shepherds, in common with some other sizable breeds, are afflicted with hip dysplasia, a hereditary disease of the joints that is both painful and crippling. No cure exists for hip dysplasia. It can be eradicated only by scrupulous care in breeding. Therefore, if you choose a German Shepherd, you should limit your dealings to breeders whose dogs have been certified free of hip dysplasia. Ask to see the certificates. Each dog is certified individually by a veterinarian.

A breeder who cares enough to have his dogs X-rayed and certified free of hip dysplasia is probably more likely to breed also for sound temperament than one who does not make that effort. In discussing temperament, Sergeant McGrogan recommended that before buying a Shepherd you ask the breeder for names of others who have bought his dogs, then take the time to check with those people as to whether they have experienced problems with temperament. The recommendation is a good one. The problem exists within the breed, or else the breed standard's list of disqualifications in conformation show competition would not conclude, as it does, "Any dog that attempts to bite the judge."

At their best, German Shepherds are magnificent dogs. Stories abound of their intelligence and loyalty, how this dog stays always between the child and the street traffic, how that one is always unobtrusively between his lady and the strange visitor ("and

nobody taught him, he just figured it out himself!'').
The varieties of tasks for which they can be trained
are legion.

Legends multiply also about Collies, traditional
protectors of the hearth. Innumerable children have
been pulled back from imminent danger by countless
Collies. Collies are about as big as German Shepherds. Their smaller cousins, the Shetland Sheepdogs, fit better in today's often limited living
quarters. Both can be superb working dogs—easily
taught, eager to please, completely loyal. They are
deservedly popular breeds, and many of them suffer
the consequences. Both have been bred without
regard to temperament. Poor temperament in
Shelties shows up as excessive timidity or shyness,
while in Collies poor temperament takes the form of
extreme nervousness, to the point of hysteria. Both are
long-coated breeds that require care (although there is
a Smooth Collie, not often seen). Both are also afflicted
with something called ''Collie eye'' (or ''Sheltie
eye''—the terms are synonymous). This is a genetical-
ly transmitted eye defect that, in severe form, causes
blindness; there is no cure. Incidence is believed to in-
crease with breeding aimed at producing smaller eyes
than would ordinarily be found in the breed.

A good alternative choice, if a Collie-type dog is
wanted, is a Border Collie, which in appearance
might be described loosely as an old-fashioned looking Collie—that is, somewhat shorter in body, not
quite as tall, and generally wider between the ears. A
good Border Collie is a nice dog.

While Collies have been loved because of ''Lassie''
and Terhune's stories about ''Lad,'' the Doberman
Pinscher has had a bad press. Used extensively as a
police and guard dog, the myth has gained credence
that all Dobes are inherently vicious. Fearless they
are, and powerful, yet they can make excellent house
and family dogs. Their official standard provides for

dismissal from the show ring for either shyness or viciousness, so both would appear to be problems within the breed. Requests for references similar to those recommended for Shepherds should uncover problem temperaments in a breeder's line.

Where Dobes command respect sight unseen on the strength of their reputation, Siberian Huskies and Alaskan Malamutes do it through appearance. Both display colors and characteristic facial markings that remind viewers uncomfortably of wolves. Siberian Huskies may possess blue eyes, which, being uncommon in other dogs, somehow suggests wildness. Malamutes are the heavier breed. Not especially aggressive, they nonetheless look ferocious. They may be roamers, so they must be controlled.

Labrador Retrievers are another good choice. They're smooth-coated dogs with a businesslike appearance, and they're as powerful as they look. Labs have been used in police and guide dog work and perform well.

An Irish Terrier might be your choice, or a Kerry Blue Terrier, both midway between Shelties and Collies in size, or possibly an Airedale Terrier, somewhat larger, almost as tall as a Collie or Shepherd. Terriers as a group are quick and aggressive and need skillful handling, but all these terriers have been used traditionally to protect the person and property of their masters.

Many Boxers go through what one breeder has described as a very long adolescence. Despite this breed trait, they have been used successfully in police work and as guide dogs. Typically, they are habitually alert, loyal to family, and wary of strangers.

Rottweilers are an old breed thought to be descended from dogs that moved with the Roman legions, whom they served by day as drovers of stock intended as meat for the troops and at night as camp guards. The modern Rottweiler still exhibits both the calm confidence of the drover and the strong guarding instinct of a natural sentry.

German Shorthaired Pointers are gun dogs used on a variety of birds and other game, including deer—all -purpose hunting dogs, as it were. As such, they typically possess good noses, a lot of endurance, and enough aggressiveness for the job at hand. They're very biddable dogs.

All the breeds mentioned thus far have been dogs of medium or larger size. No one, seeing any of them out for a walk with his master, would be in any doubt that that person was accompanied by a dog.

The ultimate size in dogdom is reached by the Irish Wolfhound. The breed history assures us that the Wolfhound would be a bad choice for a watch or guard dog on grounds of temperament: they're not sufficiently aggressive, since they're too sensitive and too loving. On the other hand, they were bred and used traditionally for hunting wolves, not easy game for dogs to bring down. Stamina and aggressiveness both were required.

One breeder of the giant hounds provided a dog door for his dogs, apparently undisturbed by the knowledge that a dog door big enough for them would accommodate a person equally well. When asked whether he worried about burglars entering through the dog door, he replied, "With all those Irish Wolfhounds waiting on the other side?" Size, by itself, commands respect.

Wolfhounds make good house dogs, better than you might suppose, but not if they must be left alone all day, every day. They are also more costly to feed than smaller dogs, their need for exercise is prodigious, and policing the premises for sanitary purposes takes on formidable dimensions. For those reasons, then, if not for temperament, some other breed might be a better choice.

Finally, if you give your heart to a Wolfhound, you must prepare to have it broken about every seven or

Reaching a height of 32 inches and weighing about 120 lbs., an Irish Wolfhound's presence can frighten would-be intruders. Photo of Pat by Ron Reagan, owned by William and Joan Gorman.

eight years, for they, along with the other giant breeds, are not long-lived. Still, it's hard to imagine anyone being assaulted while walking an Irish Wolfhound.

Great Danes are another of the giant breeds whose great size affords an always-visible deterrent. The smooth, muscled body, the free but controlled gait, the massive head, the awesome jaws all speak eloquently of great power. In common with other smooth-coated breeds, Danes look like dogs that go into action without fooling around, which indeed they do. They were developed in Germany for hunting boars, and boar hunting is not for the weak and faint of heart. Logistics of the Great Dane's care are the same as for the Irish Wolfhounds. Danes share also the characteristic of being a relatively short-lived breed.

Bigness is not the only option, in case you're thinking purely in terms of size. If you want a dog primarily to watch your premises and give notice of anyone approaching, one of the small breeds can become your loyal companion and serve you well. When the primary need is for someone to create an uproar, the small dog in fact can do a better job than his larger kindred. Small dogs have a way of retiring under things—sofas, beds, chairs, and so on— where they bark and bark and *bark* and there's no shutting them up until the excitement is over. If the excitement is a burglar or other intruder, that trait can be just what you want. Moreover, not all little dogs are yappy and shrill. Some of them have robust voices, so that anyone within hearing range might reasonably apprehend that the waiting animal is as big as his bark.

In all fairness you should know that some little dogs bark when their people are home as much as when they are not. Master is told of every falling leaf— hence the reputation for yappiness. Well, you can train your little Fido to be quiet when you want him to be quiet, or you can be philosophical about noise, put-

Meeting other dogs builds confidence. The Irish Wolfhound and the smooth-coated Terrier are both puppies.

ting up with it when you don't want it for the sake of those times when you do want it. All life is a trade-off. People living alone are prone to reach that conclusion and count it a good bargain. If they also turn their dogs into real nuisance barkers, they may tend to move a lot, one step ahead of complaining neighbors.

Pekingese dogs are natural watchdogs. They are known not to run away from other dogs and strangers.

Bermuda and SCA Ch. Fairstar Cho-Sun, Tibetan Spaniel, owned by Betty and Herbert Rosen, Bet R Kennels, Lutherville, Md. These little dogs stand about 10 inches tall. A Weidler photo.

Poodles are bred in a variety of solid colors and three sizes: Standard (over 15 inches), Miniature (10 to 15 inches) and Toy (under 10 inches). Photo by Art Wintzell.

For showing, any color or combination of colors is permissible in Shih Tzus. However, a Shih Tzu with a white blaze on the forehead and a white tip on the tail is preferred. Photo by Vince Serbin.

## Smaller Breeds

Most small breeds have been bred down in size from larger forebears. The Pomeranian, for instance, vivacious and sturdy, is thought to have been derived from sled dogs and herders of cattle. Toy Poodles are not even considered a separate breed, the Toy being merely the diminutive version of his Miniature and Standard brethren. Sometimes the origins are so far back as to have been lost, as with the Pekingese, a dog that came out of China in the 1860's, bringing with it its nickname of "lion dog," referring as much to fearless temperament as to appearance. Whatever the little ones' origins, however, their personalities and temperaments did not shrink with the rest of them. Those qualities have come down pretty much intact; Pekes are as sturdy, intelligent, loyal, and fearless in defense as dogs many times their size, so a Pekingese or dog of similar size could be your breed of choice.

No one should conclude from this brief survey that the breeds named here are the only ones to choose from. There are many others—spaniels and pointers and setters, hounds big and little, terriers a-plenty in all sizes, and so on. Each breed has its advocates. Neither should anyone infer that the ailments named in particular are the only ones afflicting dogdom. Rather, they are mentioned as a reminder that dogs, too, get sick on occasion and need care.

Whatever breed you are drawn to, you owe it to yourself and to the dog to find out as much as possible about that breed *before* you buy the dog. Books containing a wealth of information about virtually any breed you can think of are easily available. There is no perfect breed of dog. Any choice demands compromise of some kind or degree.

Compromise least of all on temperament. You do not want a timid dog. You want one as stable as you can find with enough aggression in its make-up to give it a decent self-respect. Beyond that there is no need to look for aggressiveness. Dogs are territorially minded. As soon as they can, they stake out what they consider to be their areas. Their instinct ever after is to guard what is theirs. By easy extension this includes their people and their people's belongings.

In general, any big dog costs more to feed than any little dog, while routine immunization and the initial cost of the dog may be essentially the same. In general, any long-haired breed calls for more day-to-day maintenance care than any smooth-coated dog. Drop or pendulous ears are more prone to ear problems than those that stand erect, and ear problems, if neglected, can become chronic, extremely painful, and difficult to get rid of. Little dogs tend to live longer than the giant breeds, which take longer to mature than the toys. That seems unfair, somehow, but there it is.

One more general observation can be made that cuts right across breed lines and applies to any dog you get. Your benefit from owning a dog—your reward, if you will —in protection, in companionship, in joy, will almost certainly be directly proportional to how much you invest of yourself in the dog.

For show purposes Beagles are divided by size: those not more than 13 inches tall, and those over 13 inches but not more than 15 inches in height.

**Opposite page:** The Poodle is the most popular breed in the United States and the favorite dog in several other countries, too. They are intelligent dogs and make good and reliable companions.

Kia swings in front of her mistress, placing herself between her and the opening door.

# What Every Dog Ought to Know

"Never send a boy to do a man's job," says the old adage. Similarly, you don't send a bumbling pup against thugs armed with guns, knives, and clubs. Now, dogs grow from pups to adulthood in about two years. (Under AKC show rules, they cease being puppies when they're a year old, but many breeds reach full maturity psychologically at a year and a half or two years, while the giant breeds commonly take three.) Unless they are taught otherwise, however, they may remain bumblers all their lives. Such an untutored dog, far from being of value for protection, is more likely to be a first-rate nuisance.

What, then, should your dog learn to avoid the nuisance label and justify its presence for protection? Well, it doesn't need many abilities, and those abilities don't have to be very unusual. Your dog should, however, be taught to do those few things dependably. Learning things only half way, so that performance every time is a guessing game, is not good. (Incidentally, the same few accomplishments that enhance a dog's value for protection also make that dog easier and more fun to live with.)

### Heeling on Lead

First and foremost, your dog should learn to walk by your side, whether your gait be fast or slow or mixed. The dog should do this on a lead, and the lead should hang loose from the collar. That is to say, the lead should be slack, with no tension between you at one end and the dog at the other.

43

The Silky Terrier (classed as a toy) is a spirited, spunky dog, said to be used on Australian poultry farms where they help control rodents. A Weidler photo of Jazzbo's Watch My Smoke, owned by Joseph and Donna Clas, Jazzbo's Silkies, Sykesville, Md.

The Miniature Pinscher is primarily a house dog, considered a small version of the Doberman Pinscher.

Donna Clas, Sykesville, Md., brushes her Silky Terrier, Jazzbo's Watch My Smoke. Any long-coated breed needs regular brushing. A Weidler photo.

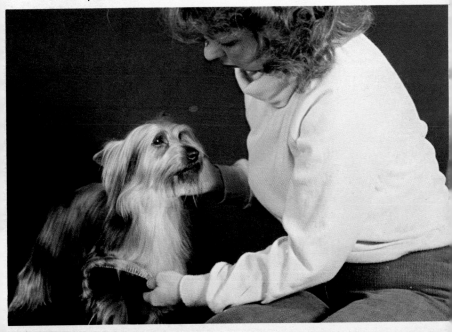

Correct heeling position. Note the following: the loose lead, the first step taken with the handler's left foot, how the handler is dressed, and the low, sturdy shoes.

This one ability, highly visible every time you and your dog leave home, will do more than anything else you can teach your dog to impress the onlooker that here is a dog under control, one that knows what it's doing. Think of the last time you saw a dog padding along beside a police officer. The dog was on a lead, and the lead was loose.

Make no mistake about it, dogs running free—more or less with their people, to be sure, but sometimes close at hand, sometimes at a distance, sniffing utility poles and lampposts and giving to their people the leftover portions of their attention—these dogs do not inspire respect. Neither does a dog lunging erratically here and there at the end of a line like a fighting fish, or tagging along a leash length behind like the tail of a kite. Any dog immediately gains in stature in the eyes of the beholder from the ability to stay with you while walking on a loose lead. In obedience circles, this is called the "heel on lead."

If you're starting, as you probably are, with a puppy that you acquired when it was from eight to twelve weeks old, you should begin your training at that early age; doing so will let you take advantage of the pup's natural stages of development. So young a puppy will naturally follow one who walks away from him. No collar. No lead. Just walk away and praise him when he follows. This is so simple that it doesn't sound much like training, but it is. Do this a few times in different surroundings, where your pup is not afraid, and your subsequent training with collar and lead will go much easier.

A good age to begin formal lead training is from four to six months. Get your plain buckle collar, put it on the dog, and leave it there. That's the first lesson. The collar should fit snugly enough that the dog can't rub it off or hook it on something. If you can slip two fingers between the collar and dog's neck, that's about right. But watch it. Pups grow fast, outgrowing collars as children outgrow shoes.

When your pup has accepted the collar—this may be in an hour, or in a few minutes, or in two or three days; be patient —he's ready for the second step. Attach the lead and let him trail it about with him. Keep a discreet eye on him, and don't leave him at home alone while he's learning to accept the presence of the

You can expect an Australian Cattle Dog puppy to develop into a strong, agile and intelligent dog. In its native country, keeping a herd of cattle or other range animals under control is required of this breed. Photo courtesy of Animals Unlimited.

**Opposite page:** Katrina Piglet Roo, O.T. Ch., T.D., owned by Helen Brigham, Silver Spring, Md. Kate is the first Australian Cattle Dog to finish as an Obedience Trial Champion. A Weidler photo.

Cocker Spaniel Carlen's Silver Sparkle ignores the lead. When your pup is similarly calm with a lead that trails, you're halfway to success in lead-breaking. However, don't leave your dog alone with a trailing leash; that could lead to trouble.

lead attached to his collar. Left unsupervised, he could get into trouble, perhaps even hang himself.

When you can see that the trailing lead doesn't bother him, pick up your end of the lead. For a day or so, go with your dog, wherever he leads. This is especially important if the early stimulation of the puppy's instinct to follow was neglected. You're letting him get used to having a tie between you, such that where one goes, the other goes also. During this brief interval while you are accompanying your dog, try to keep the lead slack. He'll know it's there, all right.

All these preliminaries should take, at most, only a few days, or you might sail through all of them in a day. Sooner or later, however, the time will arrive in your training when your dog must come with you instead of your going with him.

Correct fit of a buckled collar, shown on Cocker Spaniel M.G.M.'s Little Miss Kaplar, bred and owned by Greg Maltagliati, M.G.M. Cockers.

## The Choke Collar

Training can be made infinitely easier from here on by using a standard six-foot lead and what is known as a training collar, also called a choke or slip collar, *provided*—and it is a big proviso—that you put the collar on correctly. There are four ways to do it, so you always have a one-in-four chance of getting it right by blind luck. If you should go wrong, however, you must remove the collar from the dog and start again. No amount of fiddling with the collar on the dog will correct the mistake. Training collars, not so incidentally, are used instead of, not in addition to, other collars. Remove any leather or flea collars your dog may be wearing while you are training.

German Shepherds vary in coat color. However, rich and strong colors are preferred in show dogs. White dogs are not desirable, because they often show eye and ear defects as well.

**Opposite page:** The Border Collie is not recognized as a breed by the American Kennel Club and may not be familiar to the average person. However, they are famous all over the world for their sheepherding ability.

Making a training collar. Let the chain drop through the lower ring until the loop which you see forming is big enough to go over your dog's head.

Training collars consist of a length of chain (or nylon) with a ring at each end. The links of the chain should lie flat, presenting a smooth, even surface. If you can run your fingers along its length without feeling bumps and hollows, the chain will move smoothly and quickly in use.

Collars are sized in inches. The bigger the size, the heavier the chain. The correct size is important. Measure your dog under his throat and over the highest point of his head and add two inches. Buy the size nearest to your measurement. Too big is as bad as too little. A collar that is too small is hard to slip on and off, but one that is too big leaves too long an end after it is on the dog. A dog of no more than ordinary enterprise can learn to carry that end in his mouth, thereby frustrating the whole purpose of the slip collar.

To make a collar of this unlikely-looking object, hold one of the rings, letting the chain hang free, then grasp what has become the bottom ring (you're now holding both rings, one in each hand), and let the chain slip through the bottom ring until stopped by the upper ring. You now have a collar which can be slipped over your dog's head.

You're ready to put the collar on your dog, who is at your left side. Take a look at the collar first. It should appear like this.

Rough-coated Collies (shown here) and smooth-coated Collies are judged according to the same breed standard, except for the distribution and quantity of the coat's hair.

If held comfortably, any puppy, like this Collie, will not wriggle in discomfort but will nestle closer. Photo by Art Wintzell.

This is a female Collie being trained to grab the forearm of a would-be attacker. However, teaching a pet dog to "attack" strangers deliberately requires serious thought.

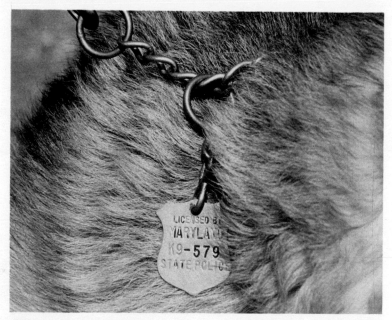

Good fit of a training collar. With your dog beside you on your left, a glance at his collar should show you this. Note the leash attached to the "live" ring, on the end of the chain which lies across the back of the neck.

Before you put it on, notice that the chain can be pulled freely back and forth through one ring which remains stationary while the other ring moves with the chain.

The collar should go on with the movable, or "live," portion of the chain lying across the back of the dog's neck. For a dog working on your left, the "live" ring should be toward your left *as the dog faces you.* The lead is attached to the "live" ring.

Now check to be sure you did it right. Pull on the lead until the collar tightens, then let go. The collar should loosen immediately. If it doesn't, take it off and try again.

The sudden change between choking tightness and comfortable looseness puts across the lessons you are teaching. Dogs do not err for long in a choice between

One way of holding excess lead, accordion-folded out of the way.

comfort, powerfully reinforced by praise, and acute though transitory discomfort unaccompanied by praise. If, however, you put the collar on upside down, as it were, it will tighten when you jerk, but it won't loosen when you let go. Every jerk simply tightens the collar still further, until you are truly choking your dog. A dog in that predicament has little chance to learn much of anything, save to fight the collar.

There seems to be a bit of mystery about putting a training collar on a dog. Some people see how it should be from the outset. Some can't get it from a book or picture but understand if somebody shows how it is done. Some people never can quite remember how it goes. No moral turpitude is involved; it's just a blind spot. Some people can never remember which way to turn the clock when the time changes in spring and

In appearance, the Shetland Sheepdog is a miniaturized Collie, 13 to 16 inches high at the shoulders. This is a working breed and breeding for a much smaller or toy size is not to be encouraged.

**Opposite page:** Naripa Blue Charm of Southlawn, Shetland Sheepdog owned by Barbara Boblick, Rockville, Md. Blue Merle is the third of the major color combinations shared by Collies and Shelties. A Weidler photo.

fall. If, however, you are in the latter group, you'll do better to abandon the slip collar and train your dog on the plain buckled collar. Training will probably take longer, but it's perfectly feasible.

*Formal Heeling*

Formal heeling, which you are about to begin, is done traditionally with the dog on your left. The dog works on the handler's left in police work, and all obedience competition follows the same convention. All the handbooks, all the training manuals, all the oral tips and tricks of the trade are grounded on the assumption that your dog is on your left, although nowhere is it chiseled on tablets of stone that dogs must heel on the left. In point of fact, numerous dogs are taught to work from either side. Dogs competing in breed classes do it routinely, where it is called gaiting instead of heeling. Still, you might as well take advantage of convention to make your dog look as professional as possible.

So get your dog on your left side, his shoulder as even with your leg as you can manage. Take a good grip on the lead. Do not, however, wrap it around your hand or slip the loop over your wrist. (There could occur an emergency when you would have to let go of the lead quickly for your own safety.) Any excess lead can be accordion-folded into either hand, but be sure that the lead hangs slack from the collar.

Now you are ready.

Give one command—only one—in the form, "Fido, heel." (Substitute your dog's name for "Fido.") As you say the words, start walking. It's important that you yourself move at the same time that you give the command. If you say the words first and then, sometime later, take your first step, there is an awkward hiatus between command and performance, when nothing happens. You and your dog stare at each other and wonder what to do next.

If he comes with you, fine; praise him. If he doesn't, give a jerk on the leash, sharp enough to make his collar uncomfortable and strong enough to bring him into position beside you. The instant he is in position, you should let the lead go slack again and praise him warmly for being where he ought to be.

To sharpen the point, Gregory Maltagliati, Gaithersburg, Md., walks right out of the picture above, leaving his Cocker Spaniel, Carlen's Silver Sparkle, behind. Many dogs give this appearance of being only nominally with the person walking them. Note also how the excess leash is wound around Greg's hand, an invitation to disaster if he should need to let go in an emergency. (Greg and Sparkle really do know how to handle themselves when a leash is between them.)

# THE WORLD'S LARGEST SELECTION OF PET, ANIMAL, AND MUSIC BOOKS.

T.F.H. Publications publishes more than 900 books covering many hobby aspects (dogs, cats, birds, fish, small animals, music, etc.). Whether you are a beginner or an advanced hobbyist you will find exactly what you're looking for among our complete listing of books. For a free catalog fill out the form on the other side of this page and mail it today.

. . CATS . . .

. . . BIRDS . .

. . . ANIMALS . . .

. . . DOGS . . .

. . FISH . . .

. . . MUSIC . . .

For more than 30 years, *Tropical Fish Hobbyist* has been the source of accurate, up-to-the-minute, and fascinating information on every facet of the aquarium hobby.

Join the more than 50,000 devoted readers worldwide who wouldn't miss a single issue.

Great Danes are alert, fearless and powerfully built giant dogs. They need plenty of exercise to maintain the muscles in good condition. Danes are available in several colors and patterns: fawn (above), brindle (top, opposite page), harlequin (bottom, opposite page), black, and blue as well. Photo of brindle Great Dane by Vince Serbin.

Praise is essential, and you have to make it sound sincere. A bored "good dog" fools no one, your dog least of all. Praise him at every flicker of response showing that the idea is beginning to register with him. Praise him also every time you let the lead go slack after a corrective jerk.

This is a matter of timing. Your aim is for the lead to hang loose from his collar *all* the time that he is in position beside you, and to be uncomfortably tight all the time that he is anywhere else. Since he is, in the beginning, apt to be anywhere else much of the time, your panicky impulse may be simply to lock your hands and hang on, while being thankful that at least the leash prevents his getting away. In consequence, your dog is merely towed about by brute force at the end of the constantly taut lead. Any praise that you might remember to utter for such a performance is meaningless, for there is no correct action to which praise can be related by either you or the dog.

As long as you don't let go, the leash does indeed prevent your dog's escape. Properly used, it does far more as a training tool. By snapping him sharply and quickly into position, and then letting the lead go slack at the same time that you praise, you have a chance to correct and praise your dog for doing what you want done, even though the length of time that he does it is, at first, no more than a moment. If every time he gets out of position he is jerked sharply back, he will come to associate the discomfort of the jerks with the fact of his being in the wrong place. His own self-interest will prompt him to stay increasingly beside you, where he can be comfortable and hear how wonderful he is.

But you do have to be decisive when you jerk. A tentative, feeble twitch does more harm than good. Keep in mind, of course, the size of your dog. A routine correction for a Wolfhound will have one of the toys airborne.

You can cause these corrective snaps to happen in

two or three ways. Bend your elbow. Put your shoulders into it and really yank. If yours is a dog who forges ahead or at a tangent to one side, turn around and walk away from him.

You'll want to practice turns and changes of pace anyway, because travel in this world is not always forward in a straight line. When you want to reverse your direction, turn always to your right, away from your dog. It's much easier for both of you. He has room to make his turn. You don't get tangled in the leash. Postpone left turns—that is, a square corner to the left—until you are both a little beyond the rank beginner stage. You might have no trouble with left turns. Then again, your dog might bump into you or crowd too close and get stepped on. If that happens, stick out your left leg while it's in the air anyway as you make your own turn. Let him walk into it as many times as need be until he learns to watch and adapt his pace to stay out of your way. This is not kicking your dog. You're setting a barrier ahead of him. Square corner turns to the right usually create no problems.

*The Sit*

When your dog shows that he is getting the idea about heeling, you can take thought for times when you have him with you but you aren't at that moment going anywhere. Either you haven't started yet, or you've stopped somewhere along the way. What should he do while you're standing still? The answer is, he should sit by your side. A dog will sit still for an extended time far more readily than he will stand still, so your control is correspondingly greater while he is sitting. You should teach him this while you perfect his heeling.

Teaching a dog to sit whenever you stop walking is relatively simple. Hold the lead with your right hand and position your left hand over your dog's back near the base of the tail. Get your hands arranged while

A Doberman Pinscher with uncropped ears. In the United States the cropping of a Doberman's ears is a routine procedure, but this is not so in other countries, like England, where the procedure is outlawed.

Fern Kowall, Scorpio Dobes, Finksburg, Md., with her red Scorpio's Impossible Dream and black puppy, Hidden Valley Tira Scorpio. Blue and fawn Doberman Pinschers are also recognized in the breed standard. A Weidler photo.

you're still moving. The instant you stop, push his rear end down to a sit and then praise him for sitting.

Resist the impulse to pull up on the leash, or he will, very shortly, think that the pull is his signal to sit. If that happens he'll wait for the pull before sitting, whereas your ceasing to move is the signal you want him to learn. In obedience competition, no verbal command cues the sit that occurs incidental to heeling. Keep your lead loose and push him into the sit. Keep at it. He'll learn.

### The Stay

The command "Fido, sit" is reserved for occasions when you want your dog to sit even though you are not at the moment walking him on lead. Frequently, after he sits, you want him to stay there for an interval, in which event the command to sit is followed by the command "Stay."

The stay can be taught in any of the dog's three natural positions—sitting, standing, or lying down. Although perhaps not immediately relevant for protection, knowledge of the stay will be handy, for it makes your dog generally easier to control. Indeed, the stay is the first thing many professional trainers teach their dogs.

In any of the positions, the stay is taught the same way. Put your dog in position, give the command to stay, and then wait an instant before praising, gradually extending the time before you praise. When your dog will stay reliably with you beside him, gradually widen the distance between the two of you. In competition the required times at the first, or novice, level are one minute for the sit, three minutes for the down, and a few seconds for the stand. The stand is not a timed exercise. The distances separating dog and handler are some 15 to 25 or 30 feet for the sit and down, but only about six feet for the stand.

Joan Zoeter leaves her Siberian Husky, Luka, on a sit-stay. Notice the hand signal that stops short of Luka's nose and Joan's first step taken on her right foot. Notice also that she starts at Luka's head so that he will *see* her first step.

The first impression that Boxers impart is their well-built and muscular bodies, and fierce expression. However, this is deceiving; Boxers are good family dogs and love children.

**Opposite page:** The Siberian Husky (top) and the Alaskan Malamute (bottom) and another Arctic breed, the Samoyed, participate in the popular sport of sled-racing in the United States. These northern breeds are equally superior as watchdogs and family pets, too. Photos by Vince Serbin.

One caveat: Don't give a stay command unless you'll be on hand to release your dog in a reasonable time. Don't try to use it, for instance, as a device to get out of the house without a fuss. He'll see through your ploy. Instead of making him steady in the stays, you'll turn him into a confirmed stay-breaker.

A word on the commands for the other stays might be in order, in case you decide to teach them also. For the stand, the command, logically enough, is, "Fido, stand," while for the down the command usually is, "Fido, down," unless you have been using "down" in a scolding situation meaning "get off the bed," "get off the sofa," "stop jumping on me," or some such. If you have used "down" in that context, then you should choose some other word—"rest" or "lie," for example—because you are not scolding your dog when you tell him to lie down.

For your present purposes, the sit-stay, taught as an adjunct to the sit while heeling, will be your most useful stay.

A dog that stays reliably and calmly by your side earns his keep at home every time you answer the door as well as out on the street.

Take him to the door with you. Take time to get him seated in a stay. Put his lead on if he's still none too steady. You aren't required to fling open the door before the doorbell echoes die. You can always call a cheery, "Be there in a minute!" if you feel that you're being too slow. When you do open the door, you should look ready and so should your dog, unflustered but ready for whatever comes. The sight of him will give many a would-be intruder second thoughts. You don't have to mention how friendly Fido really is.

## The Recall

Quite apart from any usefulness for protection—and there are obvious connections—every owner wants his dog to come when he's called; the

You aren't required to open your door wide to every stranger. Take your dog with you and be cautious until you know who's there.

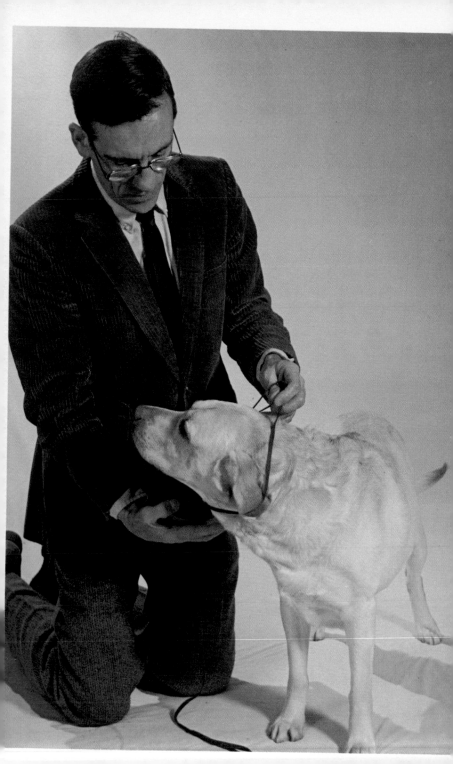

Golden Retrievers are all-around dogs. They excel in hunting and retrieving game, can be trained as guide dogs, and are naturally good and reliable companion dogs or family pets. Photo by Vince Serbin.

**Opposite page:** Charles Bacon steadies Brent-chase Maggie, yellow Labrador Retriever in the stand. A Weidler photo.

command is known in obedience circles as the recall.

If you have ever called your dog and then scolded or struck him when he reached you, it's your own fault if he doesn't come again. If a scolding is in order, you go to him. Think it over. Would you go twice to someone who called you in a friendly tone and then lit into you when you got there? Your dog is smart enough to reach the same conclusion.

With that preamble out of the way, here is a widely-used method of teaching the recall. Put your dog on a sit-stay. Back away to the end of the lead. Keep him sitting for a few seconds—vary the interval in practice—then give the command "Fido, come." At the same time jerk the lead enough to get him started, and then guide him to you, hand over hand on the lead. Be lavish with your praise when he reaches you. If yours is so large a dog that merely standing up puts him half-way to you, back away a few steps as you guide him in.

You can teach all these exercises, as they're called in obedience work, on your own at home, or you can join an obedience class. You will gain from the instructor's help, and your dog will gain from the social exposure to all the other dogs. But choose your class carefully. They aren't all good. Ask for credentials and references to other students, then check them out. Ask whether the class you have under consideration permits spectators during class sessions. Go, if it is permitted, and use your eyes.

Try to get there a little early and watch the dogs as they arrive. Do they come eagerly, tails a-wag, greeting their buddies, obviously glad to be there? One or two reluctant scholars might mean no more than timid dogs coming to class, but if the whole class, or a substantial number of the class, hang back on their leads and have to be towed in, something is going on in that class to make them feel that way. You'd best find another class.

One way to hold a dog's muzzle to stop barking. Cocker Spaniel M.G.M.'s Little Miss Kaplar, bred and owned by Gregory Maltagliati, Gaithersburg, Md., is the model.

### Barking

One of the most important protection services your dog can perform at home is simply to bark when anyone approaches. Usually a dog needs no more than minimal coaching to bark. A show of enthusiasm on your part, suitable encouragement and praise for him, and the trick is turned.

The teaching comes in training him to *stop* barking after sounding the alert. You really should make that effort; if you don't, you can very easily turn your dog into a nuisance barker.

A large part of your training problem here arises from your own ambivalent feelings. You want the dog to bark, but not too much. You're trying to teach discrimination, which is far more difficult to grasp—and not just for dogs, either—than always or never.

After his warning salvo, then, for which you have praised him, hold his mouth shut while you give him a command such as "Quiet" or "No bark" or "Stop that." Speak calmly here, and *softly*. When you let go of his muzzle after a moment or two, use the same

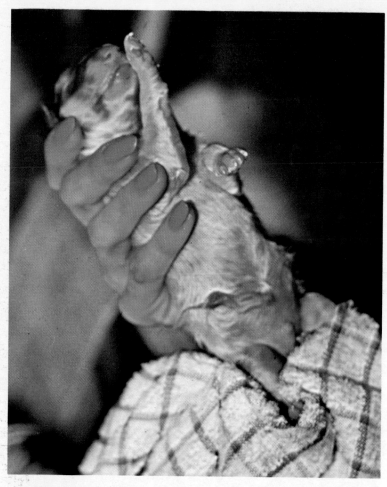

A puppy handled gently from birth encounters no socialization problems later. A Weidler photo.

**Opposite page:** Human contact enhances the taming process of any breed of dog. Shown is a Collie puppy. That a dog kept in isolation can develop behavioral problems is a known fact.

soft tones to praise him for being quiet. Gradually lengthen the time you wait before you praise.

Praise is often forgotten here because you're praising your dog for *not doing* something, whereas praise usually is ladled out as a reward for successful performance. But from the dog's point of view, he *has* done something. Two somethings. One, when he barked, and two, when he stopped. Stopping, in other words, is a positive act to him. Hence, he must be praised when he becomes quiet. Your softest tone of voice is important, too, because dogs tend to mimic behavior. "Quiet," delivered in your best full-throated bellow, will only stimulate your dog to new frenzies of barking.

If your dog is beyond your reach with his barking, he won't hear your whispers. That, of course, is why commands to cease barking are so often shouted. What you need is one sharp sound to shut him up until you can gain his attention. A slap with the flat of your hand against a door, a wall, or a table top will often do the trick. If you can clap your hands and make the clap sharp and abrupt, do that. If all else fails, try one—but only one—sudden, loud "Hey!" While he listens for that sound to repeat itself, you can reach him with your muted "Quiet!"

*Some Helpful Hints*

No matter what you try to teach your dog, you can make the training easier by observing a few general tricks of the trade much used by professional dog trainers:

1. Don't drift into the habit of making excuses for your dog. Nothing suggested in this book is beyond the reach of the most ordinary dog.

2. One-word commands are best. Decide what command you'll use for a given exercise and then stick with it. "Heel" and "let's go" and "come along" may be roughly synonymous to you, but not to your dog. Mixing up your commands mixes up your dog, too.

3. Give any verbal command one time only. From then on it's body English all the way. If you fall prey to the "sit-sit-sit" syndrome, your dog will learn to wait for all the extra commands, exactly like the child who said, "I didn't hear you until you called three times."

4. By the same token, don't use your words of command unless you're prepared to enforce them. As a practical matter, this means you have your dog on lead in active training. You want your dog to think that his obedience follows your command as night follows day. You hope he never finds out that it's possible to ignore your command.

5. Practice every day. Plan on 10 to 15 minutes at a time, twice a day, which is better than one 30-minute session. Dogs have short attention spans. At the same time, you have to be reasonable about practice with your dog. They have their good days and bad days, even as everyone else. There will be days when feelings run high and you and the dog aren't on the best of terms by the time you get to the end of one short session. If that happens, take it easy. Finish what you have started, insist that your dog do the exercise to the best of his ability, and then stop for awhile. You've had the last word. Be satisfied with that until the next session.

6. As proficiency increases, practice away from home. You can easily condition a dog to performing in one, and only one, environment or set of circumstances. You want him to be steady wherever you may be.

If attack and guard dogs are the college and high school graduates of dogdom, then your dog's attainments may justly be likened to completion of the eighth or ninth grade. He has not mastered a long list of skills, but his modest repertoire can make all the difference to you.

Of mild and kind disposition, German Shorthaired Pointers and children go well together. However, children should be warned of the consequences of maltreating any dog. Photo by Vince Serbin.

German Shorthaired Pointers perform well either as show dog or sporting dog, or both.

An Old English Sheepdog and puppy. Some owners who do not intend to show their Old English Sheepdogs often clip the coat and keep it that way all year 'round, thus doing away with time-consuming regular grooming.

A young Old English Sheepdog demonstrating his agility in clearing the broad jump. This is one of the exercises required in obedience training. Photo by Vince Serbin.

An invitation to steal. Robert and Judith Lumsden's Golden
Retriever, Dory, is the model.

# What Every Dog Owner Should Know

Sometime during your course of training you may find that you and your dog are stuck. You have been practicing faithfully, following with meticulous attention the instructions from your book or the teacher of your class, or both. Yet you make no progress. Fido's obtuseness seems extraordinary, even for him. If anything, he's going backward, growing dumber by the day. Doesn't the blasted dog have a *duty* to learn what you're trying to teach him?

Well, perhaps. But what of reciprocal duties that you may have—what about what you owe the dog?

*Protecting Your Dog's Health*

Most people recognize an obligation to maintain their dogs in good health insofar as possible. A wealth of information pours forth in an endless torrent to help you do just that. The printed word, other knowledgeable and concerned dog owners, your veterinarian—all address themselves to your questions without stint. If you will make it your habit to ask your veterinarian first, instead of as a last resort, about any health problems that develop, your vet will be grateful and so will your dog, for problems that do confront you will generally be less severe and of shorter duration.

You are more likely to receive your dog's protective services for the extended time you hope for if you take thought for his protection as well as your own. Leaving him alone is an engraved invitation for someone to steal him. Therefore, neither leave him alone in your yard, nor in your car. Thieves have gone

This photo demonstrates the power of the impact of a grown Boxer's lunge on his trainer, who is almost caught off balance.

**Opposite page:** (Top) Most dogs are easy to train, like this Sheltie sitting quietly for the trainer's command. Photo by Vince Serbin. (Bottom) This young Doberman is visibly resisting his trainer's commands. This is the time to apply the corrective jerk technique of the leash discussed in the text. Photo by Vince Serbin.

The windows are closed and the car is in the sun. Never do this to your dog. Ch. Carlen's M.G.M. Grande, the model (Gregory Maltagliati, breeder-owner) was released as soon as the picture was taken, but the car was already heating up.

into fenced yards and have broken car windows in order to steal dogs left untended. Also, don't hitch him to a post outside the store while you go inside to shop. In some parts of the country dog stealing has assumed the dimensions of a growth industry.

Life expectancy for a dog shut in a car in summer is counted in minutes. It matters not that you left all the

Airedales are used in some countries for hunting game, including large game. They are strong guard dogs and can perform police work, but are also excellent house pets.

**Opposite page:** Teal's Radiant Sun-Shine, Pomeranian, owned by Patricia Teal, Westminster, Md., takes time out with young Joshua Teal. A Weidler photo.

Food refusal is an extension of "No." Teaching is easier if you can enlist a friend to help, someone not a member of your household. Your dog accepts food, quite properly, from members of your family. Whether feeding is limited to food in his dish at mealtime or includes tidbits from the table is up to you. In any event, your dog already knows that food is all right when offered in association with the scent of any member of your family. Recruiting an outsider to help removes one possible source of confusion for your dog.

Your helper acts as tempter, offering food from the hand and also placing it on the ground or floor where it can easily be found. With your best "No" you forbid the taking. Be lavish with praise at your dog's first sign of retreat from the goodie.

Dogs can be so conditioned in this manner that they will starve themselves before accepting food from a stranger. It's a good idea, therefore, when he is steady in refusing food from your helper, to take him a step further and teach him that accepting is all right if, and only if, you give express permission first.

*Your Dog's Mental Health*

In addition to your dog's physical safety, you should consider his mental well-being.

Play fair. If you expect him to watch the house while you're away, leave him in the house with the interior doors open so he can make his rounds. How can he guard the house while tied to a stake in the back yard or confined to the tool shed? If burglars load your possessions onto a truck and then you blame your dog for not preventing what he could not get near, he will understand only that you are capricious and hard to please.

An honest effort to see matters from your dog's point of view will sometimes dissipate training problems before they arise. If your dog watches with benign interest as the playful scuffling grows pretty rough around the house, don't immediately conclude that he will watch with the same kindly eye while muggers beat you senseless. Your dog knows that you are in no danger from the horseplay. He registers with nice discrimination your lack of fear in the first instance and reacts to the real, instead of the apparent, situation. An animated dog may join the game, but he will be playing, too.

Now about getting stuck. If you train long enough, you'll find this happening at irregular intervals. It's a part of training that happens to everybody. Progress is a series of plateaus, not a ramp pointing ever upward. The solution is to keep on practicing. You'll be glad you did.

Behind the ferocious image of a modern Bulldog is a mild and sweet disposition. But, when necessary he will defend his master as tenaciously as his bull-baiting ancestors did more than a hundred years ago.